A FRESH FOOTPATH

My New Life in Poetry

By GEORGE S. CHAPPELL

Ellie,

Best wishes.

George Chappell

Cover photo by the author:
A footpath at Goddard College
in Plainfield, Vermont

PELL PRESS
2011

A Fresh Footpath
My New Life in Poetry

Some poems have been published in
The Bangor (Maine) Daily News
and
Cupola of Moses Brown School
Providence, RI

Available directly through
Pell Press
and
www.createspace.com/3674450

Pell Press
Post Office Box 4,
Rockport, Maine 04856

George Chappell's unassuming lyrics unfold memories of a boyhood marked by bewildering uprootings; a sense of hard-won reconciliation achieved years after the death of a difficult father; and an attachment to the local environment that makes an apple tree with its moss-patterned trunk as familiar to the poet as human kin. Threaded with sorrow, wistfulness, joy, and wry humor, these poems balance their investment in the richly evoked past with nicely judged attention to the present. Charting a course that is both wide-ranging and circumspect, *A Fresh Footpath* movingly fulfills the speaker's desire to throw off his culture's blinkered utilitarianism and take up residence in the community of artists.

> Jan Clausen, Poet
> *If You Like Difficulty*
> *From a Glass House*

The world is a better place for George Chappell's skillfully crafted poems, for his restrained yet clear-eyed observations, whether his subject be war, atrocity, love or a moose and his dog. His honesty, his complicated goodness and his restrained sharp humor shine through these poems, scraping us clean, calling on us to see our own lives with the same subtlety, clarity, and decency.

> Nicola Morris, Poet and teacher
> Ithaca, New York

This book is dedicated to

DOUGLAS HALL
1938—2011

Friend, poet and teacher,
of Windsor, Vermont.

Acknowledgments

Many thanks to the faculty at Goddard College in Plainfield, Vermont, especially my advisors Nicola Morris and Jane Wohl, who gave me continuing encouragement and advice to complete my Master of Fine Arts degree and this manuscript. Thanks also to poet and Goddard College teacher Jan Clausen for her efforts as a second reader of my manuscript. Thanks to my close friend Judy Orne Shorey of Rockland, Maine, for our ongoing conversation of poetry and poems in progress, and to Judy Knowlton, my "Bookbuilder."

Special thanks to Kathleen Ellis, poet and teacher of the art and poetry workshop at the Farnsworth Museum in Rockland.

I am indebted to the works of William Stafford, Gary Snyder, Mary Oliver, Robert Frost, Charles Simic, Emily Dickinson, John Milton, John Keats, Yusef Komunyakaa, Robert Hayden, Stanley Kunitz, Mark Doty, Wesley McNair, Annie Dillard, Kenneth Koch, Adrienne Rich, and Wallace Stevens.

A special acknowledgment goes to my late wife, Inger Larsen Chappell, and to my four sons, George, Geoffrey, Jon and David, for putting up with my lifetime passion for poetry.

TABLE of CONTENTS

PART ONE

PART Two

PART *Three*

PART ONE

A Challenge to Find One's Way

When I read Robert Frost's sonnet, "Into My Own," I found that the couplet at the end of this poem awakened something in me, as if in 1913, when he published the verses, Frost had written the last two lines about my life: "They would not find me changed from him they knew—/ Only more sure of all I thought was true" (5). Poetry hits the mark when it strikes a reader's personal note.

"Into My Own" is the first poem of Frost's original collection, *A Boy's Will.* The title is a line in Henry Wadsworth Longfellow's, "A boy's will is the wind's will," from *My Lost Youth.* (Oxford 316).

I don't believe that Frost in borrowing the phrase intended to talk about his youth, for that's not what his poem is about. It's really about forging his way into the future with confidence in himself. My identification with the final couplet is not about my youth, either, lost or otherwise. The sentiment behind the couplet is that old acquaintances or loved ones will not find one changed, but only more sure of oneself and more self-confident than ever.

I felt the couplet spoke to me because at this stage of my life I'm on a path of my own, regaining values and interests of my youth, which I had put away in my middle years, and finding my own way back with self-confidence.

The speaker of Frost's poem says the old trees in the forest are strong and dark from which he wants to steal away. He is unafraid of the future, "Fearless of ever finding open land," and willing to push on to a life at the edge of doom, because life behind him is dull and monotonous, "where the slow wheel pours the sand."

Frost's thesis becomes a challenge to me in my first book of poems because he speaks in a bucolic metaphor that I share and sets a high poetic standard for me to attain. I humbly would like to consider him as my mentor. He was one of the first poets I read as a child. From his poem here, I can see that he and I have had in common the inner struggle to gain confidence in our own beliefs. That's a struggle worth having and winning.

Frost, Robert. *The Poetry of Robert Frost*. New York: Holt, Rinehart and Winston, 1969.
Darwin, Bernard, ed., *The Oxford Book of Quotations*, 2nd ed. London: Oxford University Press, 1953.

Pioneering in a Life of Poetry

The path to the library becomes less stony
with every step away from the parking lot,
where a life of wheeling has dogged my years.

I would sell my car to the first buyer,
and take my stand against exhaust fumes
as a statement on leaving my old ways,

vestigial of the worn path others
groomed for me, for a new footpath,
feathered with fresh pine needles,

following my new job of poetry,
testing my voice and skills
with some poets I admire:

Whitman, Stafford, Snyder, Frost, Stevens.
With my each new line a past failure goes
              down,
healing my conscience and renewing my
              faith.

First Leaving

I wander around my yard at dusk
under an elm's bare branches.
Shadows shade a white fence, barrier
between the road and my scooter rides.

To the right, by the garage, grownups plod,
packing a car that looks already full.
Lights shine through the windows of our
        house
revealing empty rooms and half-drawn
        shades.

This noon, two men arrived in a van,
and my father led them to my bedroom,
whereupon they loaded my furniture,
my toy box, and my buddy, my scooter.

I had asked my mother where our family
was going: *Your father has a new job in Vermont,*
she said. *We have a new house there.*
Would Grandma, who lived up the road,
        come, too?

Grandma will stay behind in Rhode Island.
The Halloween air is turning to a chill.
I've said goodbye to one friend,
but I still need to talk to Peanut,

my skinny seven-year-old playmate from
        school.
We spend hours riding scooters
and catching frogs near the pond
behind my house.

(more)

My family doesn't seem to like her,
never invites her to my birthday parties.
Peanut's father is in the war in France,
and she lives with her mother in a cabin.

My grandpa used to tease me about her:
Her clothes reek, and she always picks her nose,
he would say. I pretended not to hear,
and that was my way of backing my friend.

But this time I feel alone and scared,
knowing we are shutting down the house,
and I won't see my friends ever again.
Hey, Silly, over here, a voice whispers.

I turn to look to the voice and see her.
Here, Peanut says, handing me a pearl knife,
with a rusty serrated blade for scaling fish
as if she knows I will find fish galore.

Grasping, I hold her fingers in the night;
we stare at one another and say nothing.
*Come on. Let's go. We've got
a ten-hour drive,* Dad calls.

Moving to Vermont

Trudging up School Street hill
past the brick building with a fire escape
and gnarled sugar maples,
I head to the ball field beyond
to my new schoolmates

gathering along the third base line,
now hidden under fresh January snow.
They are ready for me
the new kid, moved
to town for a family job.

Standing on the plateau above the school,
I feel my fingers tighten in my pockets.
Tradition, stronger than any human power
inside the building,
has drawn us all to the ball field.

No one has positioned us, but I stand my
    ground
on the first base line across the diamond
from the battalion between third and home;
a silence settles over the field

(more)

of boys in ear-muffed helmets,
girls in knee-length gray coats and wool
    stockings,
breathing steam into bright red mittens.
Without a word, the boys reach down,
clasp wet snow to roll into a ball.

I'm an Alpine trooper in white uniform,
like one I'd seen in a war photo,
who could defy the odds against an army.
I fire back, one snowball at a time.

The barrage from third base continues
for another minute, and stops.
The boys run to tell me I'm okay.
The girls look down as the school bell rings.

The Messenger

I'd drop down to my front toe line
       head up, chest aquiver
eager for the race's start,
       while crowds made me shiver.

My fists would gouge into the turf
       to poise me for the run,
sometimes I saw the pistol's puff,
       at times I heard the gun.

O, how often I've pushed with pride
       the rivals at my back,
breathing hard, not losing stride,
       to break free from the pack.

Though they call me Pheidippides
       you may not know my name;
after the brave soldier from Greece
       who died not seeking fame,

while running the twenty-six miles
       over Marathon's plain,
to tell Athens and all the world,
       of the rout of Persians.

In my races, I feel his mind,
       my chest puffed in prowess
to float under a boost of wind,
       his gift grown effortless.

The Stare

Seagull, staring at sky from the ground,
why did you come into range,
of the little boy's stone, hurled
while you rested in his yard?

The boy ran away, after witnessing
what he had wrought, terrified,
because he sensed the life force
was gone from you, leaving the stare,

indifferent as all nature usually is.
Did the boy wonder about the result,
that he had killed something? Did he know
what the word *killed* even meant?

Later, the boy told his father
about you, Seagull, lying still
in your gray and white feathered
calling hours coat. The boy cried

when he told the tale of a rock
as big as a baseball
thrown true to the mark,
in surprise, of an unknown skill.

PART TWO

Sojourner in the Countryside

Driving a back road by the North Branch,
where not a ripple shows under the sun,
I slow while a woman crosses patiently
to her mailbox. She appears to feel safe.

As if to make certain, she turns her head
while clutching her mail, and looks straight
            at me
through my windshield. I look back, hesitant,
feeling like a homesick boy, but really

a 50-year-old man under the spell of summer
            sun.
In my mirror, I see her turn her head
to her yard, an isolated home
of house, fence and barn—her haven or jail?

I marvel at the adolescent stalks
of corn just beginning to tassel
across the way, down to the river's edge
where I see three boys swim from a sand bar.

I know at that moment if I stop
the car, I will be fourteen again.

Facing John Cheever at His Grave

Photo by Austin Borror-Chappell,
grandson of George Chappell

18

There lies John Cheever under a black
    tablet,
next to his parents, in the First Parish
Cemetery, Norwell, Massachusetts.
Was he a good man to want to do that?
To be buried in the same plot as they?
When I asked my grandson to drive me
    there,
he agreed, having just got his license,
welcoming a chance to show me his skill.

Who was Cheever, and why was he special?
My grandson asked. That he was a famous
    writer was an easy reply.
How could I make clear
what his attempts to heal his drunkenness
meant to my addiction—
why Cheever's life could help me stop
    drinking?

Song of the Osprey Realm

On a July morning years ago,
my friend and I launched a boat
framed in sheets under nimbus clouds
to make off for a sail on the Chesapeake.

Tacking and bum tacking along a creek
we cut away to a channel marker
past a shoreline of weeping willows,
dreamily drooping in their sunbath.

It was a day to exorcise ghosts
          a day without the blues
          a day to be played in the key of C.

A guest to these waters, I noticed
an osprey nesting in a steel basket,
on top of a rolling channel marker,
selecting and nipping his stalks of straw.

An Eastern Shore girl, my friend told me
ospreys used to nest and flirt in the marsh,
before house developers drove them out.

So there my osprey sat in composure,
a scruffy bird with unerring vision
to survive, when it flicked through the water
and emerged with a wriggly, walleyed catch.

(more)

From far off a bow seemed
to sound a purl from a cello
over waves to go with music,
reminding me of endless time.

I daydreamed a nest peerage on the bay:
	with the ghostly ospreys in pantomime
	laughing in reproach toward the shore.

Sonnet of the B-52

Here, while passing cars slip in snow below,
giant bombers dip and soar overhead,
doing their dance while they circle targets
before coffee is served in the war room.

Sky games at Loring keep pilots astute
in war machines, practicing over fields,
for combat against Bedouin warriors
on Arabian steeds of desert lore.

Just for today, pilots play maneuvers,
flying relics of nuclear fission,
averting entry into scrap storage.
So, soar, O Great Planes, find your position.

Just for now, B-52s dart and dip;
time moves to ground you where Bedouins
        failed.

Corn Dog Phobia

Summer time brings the scent of corn dogs,
pleasant to most, but not to Frank,
who says the smell now makes him sick.
Frank's father took him as a boy
to see a film on submarines,
The Hunt for The Red October.

On a cool night in October
after I consumed four corn dogs,
I saw the moving submarine
and felt nauseous, says Frank.
Even the hint of a dog to the boy,
was cause enough to make him sick.

In grade school, he says, *I'd get sick*,
reminded of the sight of *October*.
How motion could upset that boy!
Something about the smell of corn dogs
something about the sight of those franks,
stirred up buried fears of submarines.

The motion of the submarine
simulated from the film the sickness
observers saw with each frank
a review of panic that *October*
made something happen to the dogs,
when paired with the appetite of the boy.

(more)

When food was scraped from trays, the boy
said he felt the motion of submarines
and recalled the time he stuffed dogs
in a hurry to make him sick.
He searched for his own *October*
to understand his fear, said Frank.

Fear comes from fear itself, said Frank
Roosevelt. What turned a schoolboy's
stomach was sight of *October's*
sea motion of a submarine
and recall of the day he was sick
from eating too many corn dogs.

Time to put away sickness, says Frank.
Now *Red October* hunts for other submarines,
and the boy-man learns to ignore corn dogs.

Morning Prayers

When I first heard the priest, a mouse crept
    by,
its eyes darted side to side, its nose shook,
as it witnessed the people at worship,
then burrowed its head between its paws.

While the priest prayed, I saw an ambulance
from up the street drive by, its flashing lights
altered the pre-dawn blackness into gray
to illuminate unfolding brown fields.

After the priest was done, a red fox ran
from the woods and headed toward the
    fields,
distracting the mouse inside, pondering
how it might have been in an old era,

before ambulance, houses or highway
existed, or priests donned their frocks to
    pray.

Blueness of Blue

Looking at William Zorach's *Bay Point,*
an oil paint wash and watercolor on paper,
I see no *unravished bride of quietness*,
only four humpbacked islands

protruding from an ocean
shaded bluer than blue.
While I'd like to see a bride to ravish
in a painting, the fullness of Zorach's

blue water captivates me to hold on
to what else might be,
when my life longs for passion:
I see mysterious scratches on the beach,

a lighthouse atop one island, a home
crowning another, but no people,
only etches in the gray sand
by the cove showing signs of life.

I look again and see white spray
on the rocks and a red buoy marker.

Tribute to Kenneth Koch

Kneeling like a serendipity buff
before my scratched
walnut brown bookcase,

I poke through volumes
left from other decades
by friends and loves gone by.

A true believer in books,
I let my fingers choose
a paperback poetry book,

Thank You and Other Poems
by the late Kenneth Koch
(whose name sounds like bloke).

A two- and three-quarter inch
by one- and one-half inch receipt,
giving no name or place of business

but a *Thank-You* at the top,
and a *Call-Again* at the bottom,
bearing a two-dollar and nine-cent

price tag, serves as a bookmark.
I submit that Koch would relish
saving such a coincidence

(more)

as his title and gratitude
for buying his book in Manhattan
on a summer night in 1972,

when I walked the city
alone, feeling its pulse,
confronting new poetry.

As I write, white butterflies
move in fluttering gestures
above the browning rye

across from my Maine home.
No breeze hinders their flight
over farmland left for grazing.

Koch would ask for a voice
from the field to cry out
what it's like to be rye grass,

a butterfly to say how
it feels to be a butterfly,
or a rose where it gets its red.

Unconditional Love

At the first curve
of mountain road
she came to attention
in my car,
chin up, eyes front,
nose straight ahead
stone-still beside me.

A moose loomed
into view, uncertain,
as usual, of its direction—
I sped past, and beagle
nose snapped to her side window
barking ferociously.

It's all right now, I said,
patting her silky ears and head.
The nose quieted down.
We were safe again.

Seasoned Hearts

I'd ask John Donne to summon his powers
   to *batter my heart*
for you, but it's been repaired so often, I
   don't know
if even his god can piece it together at my
   age.

Why don't we just take a ride together
   through the countryside
on a train dining car with wine glasses on the
   tables
to romance our seasoned state?

The wine would help us forget our scars in
   strange
places where only we can see them
in moments of intimacy—but that's all
      right—

I with my thin surgical line on my breastbone
   where they sliced me open,

and you with an electronic pacer
beating time to your own rhythm—
or is that the vibration of the train?

I sit across the table from you,
not touching my wine, just holding your
   hand,
daydreaming.

On the Train to San Francisco

She sleeps on the bunk below me
on the cross-country train to San Francisco:
oblivious to passing landscapes:
industrial buildings pale and wan
under fading sodium lights.

The train slows for Cleveland at 3 a.m.
Fog shrouds boat silhouettes
tied to docks on Lake Erie.
The Browns' football stadium
looms into view
so close you could touch
the team's lettering on the curved wall.

On my feet now, I straddle the aisle
Wake up! I say. *We're in Cleveland.*
But she doesn't oblige.
She's slowed into her own reverie.

Holding on

Old maple trees lean out over our home
on the river, but, like us, they don't break,
rather, they extend their leafy dome
over nesting herons we found awake

in shadows, shielding warm corps
of fledglings that cried into the stillness.
Winds rippled cross-currents between stream
     shores,
as if to mark the renewed life in our place.

Once, we lost our way and let others
take us, and we bobbed like buoys upon
     swells,
hope fading while what we had seemed less,
until we chose to call back our own
     farewells.

This time, we push the surge our way;
This time, we work to make the love stay.

Living on the breath

Words live on the breath
                    —Jane Elkington Wohl

The woman lay dying
on her living room sofa,
her family gathered around:
husband, children and grandchildren,
there were eight altogether,
leaning over her, trying to get close.

The family had kept a watch all night
not wanting to miss a moment
of this woman's life
before she left the world.
She was 65 but looked much younger
          in her repose

Never a morning person,
she must have resented
being called at 9 a.m., her official time,
though she'd always risen early for a trip.

A hospice nurse lingered
in the background, keeping
a respectful distance from the grieving
          family.

The dying woman had asked
to leave her bed the night before
to be brought to the living room,
It was her proper role for one last time
to greet her guests to her home.

(more)

41

Her moment of death neared,
her breath rattled with each draw,
she looked up at her husband,
her eyes wide open, whites showing
as their eyes met for a moment,
and then she closed hers.

Sensing death, the relations around her
told her in a chorus of their love
for her. *I know*, she whispered,
as she exhaled for the last time,
the words floating from her lips.

Sweet Lingering Scent

The crumpled cigarette pack in the glove
    box
of her black Volkswagen stirs my mind,
weary from her memorial service.

I reach for her pack, lift it to my nose,
catch a whiff of her lingering,
and recall old spats about smoking,

when she'd say *they*
would find a cure
before she got old.

PART THREE

Will lilacs Bloom at My Lai?

In a certain dooryard, where a lilac bush stands,
people flock to see if the bloom has come back
But the bloom has withered from the bush
and no peace dove sings.

We all recall your stovepipe hat, Abe,
the symbol of a war victory
that cost you your life
and gave you a long train trip in state.

I've wondered, do you presidents gather
in heaven to compare notes
on your accomplishments?

Since most presidents conduct wars,
I would imagine you'd have moments
of asking forgiveness,
like attending a presidential AA meeting:

Hello, my name is Abe Lincoln,
and I'm a grateful recovering
presidential statesman.

Have you met Lyndon Johnson?
You and Lyndon have presidencies in
    common:
You freed the slaves, and he gave them
civil rights 100 years later.

Do you remember General Sheridan,
whose Union soldiers plundered Virginia
    farms
shooting women and children
while the men were at war?

(more)

A century later, Lieutenant William Calley
went with troops to a Vietnamese village,
    called My Lai,
to shoot Vietcong, but the men weren't
home when he got there.

Calley's troops gathered the women, children
and elderly at My Lai and shot them
as they huddled together,
like bundles of cornstalks,
just before their execution.

Two photographers with him
snapped pictures of the victims
seconds before they were killed
so that you could see the terror
in Vietnamese faces at the exact moment.
Those pictures came back to indict Calley.

Let's hope that soon you presidents will have
run out of wars to discuss at your meetings,
and you can focus on having peace
in your recovery.

We'll know,
when your lilacs bloom again.

Stalking the Home Diamond

Waking up alive in Maine Medical Center
after heart surgery,
I saw my four sons grinning at me
from the foot of my bed.

From where we were, nine stories up,
we looked out the window to see
a ballpark with seagulls
sauntering across centerfield,
their heads turning side to side
in the July sun, stepping deliberately,
white and graceful, against the grass.

Years earlier, my father lay sick
in this same hospital, watching
that ballpark being built,
hoping to see a game there.

At the Psychiatrist's Parking Lot

A blinding sun
in a November afternoon
highlights cold, brilliant
late green lawns,
dead leaves in corners
of porches, among tree roots,

while big, rumpled, ungainly self seeks

spiritual relief,
where soup kitchen sign
on nearby church
points to basement saying,

Use back door, please.

Reconciling

July 7, 2009

Today would have been
your ninety-second birthday
we might have made peace by now,
but I used to step gingerly
around you.
Your voice was a snarl—
Did you see something
in me that you wanted to drive out?

A child of the Great Depression,
you were driven to succeed.
We moved so many times
to satisfy your need for success—
I hated every move.

Yet, when I thought contact
between us was hopeless, you called me
long distance to tell me you were sorry
Elvis had died. I was touched by your call.

Years later, after your business dream failed,
you taught me a lesson by picking
up your life and going on.
To you, there was no other choice.

Grandma once told me that as a boy
you saved someone from drowning,
and your town gave you a medal.

Wordsworth said it best:
Your youth became father to the man.

Sanctuary

(For Tom O'Donovan, creator of Harbor Square Gallery, Rockland, Maine)

After harvesting a green tomato just before
      a frost
scraping kernels from my one ear of corn
to show for a whole season
of growing in the rain and mud

I stroll on the harbor boardwalk, near
where a sculptor bought an old bank
converting it to a gallery
planting a rooftop garden four floors up

filling it with terracotta statues:
a thinker pondering the Universe
scratching his chin
a woman tending her dollhouse garden

with a Mistress Mary watering can.
I go walking about the neighborhood
seeking my play within a play
hoping to find my conscience.

(more)

I go deep into my own wild, back
for sustenance into the gallery where Cato,
the sculptured black walnut cat,
reposes with front paws curled

under him, guiding me
back to the rooftop garden
to awaken me to my vision
gleaned before the harbor beyond.

Burial at Sea

I push off in my dory, against
my better judgment, with two tourists
and their homemade wooden urn
to empty their relative's ashes at sea.

One occupant looks stern enough
to intimidate armies. She says she will write
a book about the deceased
before gardening time—an air of confidence

about planting, less so for writing.
I wish you'd speak up, she tells
her friend, who is reciting burial prayers
over the wind and engine noise.

I can see out beyond the breakwater:
two sailboats lean windward
in roiling waters turned slate gray
in October winds, a time fishermen

hesitate before putting out from land
on an ocean rough enough to capsize
a boat carrying even sturdy tourists,
who misconstrue respect for the sea

for laziness or cowardice. I head my boat
into the waves, while the two bearers
in a stalwart stance against the blow
cast the urn's ashes into our faces.

Apple Tree with a Mossy Crotch

From my kitchen it's 500 feet to my apple
    tree
I sit in the morning, hands wrapped around
hot coffee, cars on the road behind me

hurtling to jobs in town a mile away.
I notice my apple tree has a blemish of moss
facing me north under its crotch

with two branches pointed up,
not down – my tree won't walk away,
and I couldn't stop it if I wanted to.

Four years ago I moved into this house
to grieve alone someone I'd lost,
and my beagle to help me.

Then my beagle died and I had a
lawnmower, southbound geese
in the fall, a vegetable garden

in spring and my thoughts always.
Why on this morning do
I notice this tree for the first time

after four years of looking
out on the yard daily?
Does this tree have a name?

Has it decided after four years
to make my acquaintance
and show me its mossy crotch?

Lunch at the Graveyard

Here we are in daylight on the island,
spending an afternoon
seated at our picnic for two
by your grave, and you're waiting

for my preparation to celebrate your life,
with deviled eggs and tanqueray martinis,
placed on your mother's faded wedding cloth
in the cemetery where we first made love.

Remember fifty years ago, when we would
        leave
your parents' home for a moonlight walk?
We held hands and felt the fog on our faces,
not needing the flashlight we carried.
Our youthful steps were nimble in the grass,

and you said the fog was good for a girl's
complexion, sounding as true
as anything you said, made more pleasing
by how you said it in your Maryland drawl.

Our lunch is an anniversary of sorts,
to boost memories after the years
since your death, as if to let go
of your ghost would end reality.

There's your old neighbor passing by.
She's looking oddly at my solitary picnic,
and waving hesitantly from the path.

I'll wave back and begin the trudge toward
        shore
to cross the bar before low tide strands me.

Homage to Annie Dillard

In sharing with my students,
   Pilgrim at Tinker Creek,
      bearing a cover photo

of its author, Annie Dillard,
   perched on a rock by the stream
      where she explored and meditated,

I had hoped to awaken
   them to her natural world,
      to have them walk along her ridge

and know her experience,
   to meet her feisty tomcat, and to gather
      for meteor showers from the heaven
         of Walt Whitman.

But, when asked about the book,
   students didn't know the answers
      for they hadn't read the homework.

I had thought they were kindred spirits
   whose love of nature was like mine,
      and that we sought a cleaner world

that Annie Dillard wanted, too.
Now I stood, puzzled, in the classroom
while they apologized to me.

I recalled Whitman's poem
about the *learn'd astronomer*,
and the man who left the lecture hall.

and walked off by himself
in the mystical moist night air
to look up in perfect silence at the stars.

Then, my students and I left our classroom
and walked outside on the spongy earth
to ponder the flow of a nearby stream.

George's Spirit Watches over the Moores

George, the black lab guardian of the Moores
of Port Clyde, Maine,
watched over them and their home
ever reminding them to close the mud room
    door
even though his eyes could no longer see.
He always knew his family when it came and
    went,

and he liked walking to shore to bark at gulls.
Now his spirit hovers at night, ready to fly
    south
to Hilton Head, South Carolina, for future
    winters
at the family's other home.
His once lame and wracked dog body,
too sick to make the trip in life,
required him to be left behind.

He waited this spring for the Moores' return
    to Port Clyde,
giving the family one last nuzzle
before he settled in with a sigh on his favorite
    rug.

BP Oil Spill: Gulf of Mexico, April 2010

(after scene in a New York Times *photograph)*

Clean-up crew members talk on the beach
and pick up dead gulls and pelicans,
as the tide hisses out to its ebb,
exposing more and more bird bodies.
The men do not seem to count the carcasses
but take them one by one and put them
into a construction debris bag until full.
They overlook a crane, lying on the sand,
its brown sticky down coated with tar,
its neck outstretched, bill sealed, eye staring.

Kristallnacht:

What a Tinkling Sound!

Tell me where all the details have gone
 from the Night of the Broken Glass
 in Germany and Austria,
seventy-two years ago.

Nobel Laureate Elie Wiesel
warned us never to forget
what happened on those two nights
November Ninth and Tenth, 1938,
when Nazis broke windows

of the homes and businesses
of Jews, killing many—
passing laws,
disenfranchising Non-Aryans,
marking the start of the Holocaust.

At home in America, years later, we wait
while watching new hooligans, who break
    no glass,
but who carry arms in the name
of a document, handcuff and threaten
journalists at rallies and shout down
    opponents.

Thugs throw a gay man named Charlie off a
    bridge to drown,
try to deprive children education and
    medical care,
and deny the tired and poor a haven.

Now we hear the snarls again,
and still we look for the smoke
to tell us there's a fire.

The Thrill of It All

The flats lie low at night like a swamp
suffused with tidal smells, met at the edges
by high water. Only drivers disrupt
the quiet of night as they quicken on their way.

Driving a Ford convertible too fast at night
between the Scarborough marshes
is like racing with no racetrack
without a sign of another vehicle
not even a highway cop to arouse fear,
only the thrill of vibrations in the steering
    wheel,
tires trembling over road pebbles, and
the adventure of being almost out of control.

The 22-year-old blue-eyed man—that was the
age on his driver's license—
in his black convertible with red interior
blaring a rock station, must have felt
    invulnerable.
His friends said later that he never knew fear.

He mustn't have seen the tractor-trailer
coming his way, or heard its drive train
gearing down
as the truck approached the curve,
while he punched his radio buttons.

Off to his left, he might have seen
an orange glow from the harbor
and white city lights from beyond,
before they went out.

Reunion via the Providence Bus Tunnel

My classmates didn't see my flushing
   cheeks
or notice that my breath came short. They
thought it odd that I chose to ride the bus
up East Side hill to our old school, where

fifty years later, we grouped again at
central hall. But I still see the tunnel
through which long ago I biked with my girl
in her sweater and blue jeans that still cling,

her hair unfurled, in my mind's reflection,
of our races down to beat the transit.
The tunnel's old now. The busses slip
   through
pale, dingy walls, peeled from bad smelling
   fumes.

New kids fix their gaze on uphill busses,
cigarette smoke curling over their trance.

Ode to a Cruise Ship

O Great Ship that comes to port
your blast so shrill to warn all others

that deign to use the shipping lane
where your anchors dredge up

lobster traps and fishing nets.
Your entrails dumped near shore

while your propellers chew up
offal and disperse it to the fish

or break off coral to sell to tourists.
O White Behemoth of the Sea

bring forth your visitors to our land
to swarm our stores in search of trinkets

and push our people off the sidewalks.
The God of Commerce blesses you for all.

Bowing to a Gardener

When I came to a stop
at your heart, rain fell
softly on the roofs of your town,

and pollinated the night
that surrounded me,
healing a rover with its drops.

Once my life flowed over me,
imposing vows from which I ran,
but your delicate touch awakened me

to rise up and celebrate
you and your garden,
to share your quest

in warming its fields.
We couldn't get closer
in spirit or flesh than lovers

on a bitter, cold night,
made over by beauty and joy
of love for all life.

My Father's Hands

As I near my father's old age, I look
at my hands and know that they are his.

My father's hands were quick and strong.
and he used them to build me a life as a man.

Those hands taught me how to box,
do algebra homework, drive a car.

At my high school graduation,
he grinned and shook my mother's hand.

When he got old, his skin became
cracked by chemicals from his work,

although his hands still had character
to fulfill his dream as a chaplain to the sick.

His hands gave me my hands—
his were ambidextrous, mine swung left—

I used my hands to tie shoes,
first mine and then my children's,

to pray or write,
to offer or make love.

Moose in the Road

Snow is falling on the way to Jackman,
    Maine,
high in the mountains, where terrain is stark.
A moose, covered in white, lies in the road,
drawing heat from the friction of tires.

The moose rises as I start to freewheel
in my wide-track Peugeot station wagon;
never stepping on brake or gas pedal,
I hurtle downhill toward the thousand-pound

antlered beast, noted for standing its ground.
Snow veils the shadow of its looming form.
Deep roadside ditches leave no room to
    swerve,
and putting on the brakes I'd lose control.

But, that wilderness bull has other thoughts:
with a lurch and skip, it bounds away.

The Old Master: A Portrait

Grizzled in gray
on an expressionless face
he turpentines the paint,
stirs the pot, while

odors of linseed oil and spirits
mingle in his nostrils.
Rising sun burns away
cool, red rays of dawn.

He goes up a ladder,
grasping rungs,
swinging tools,
peering up at flaking eaves.

Glancing down,
where young co-workers talk, smoke,
smirk at time,
he continues to the top.

Craning his neck toward the frieze,
he begins wire-brushing crevices.
A smile crosses his face;
a flicker lights his gaze.

Granite Come Together

(after Link, 2010, *a sculpture of Sullivan granite by Jesse Salisbury at the Farnsworth Museum, Rockland, Maine)*

We are so entwined in our granite loops,
we move only when hoisted—

the sculptor's powerful hands
split us from our mother block at the quarry

fashioned us as one
like twins at birth, joined

to make an eight-foot bridge,
two pillars combined

around our other part,
a large stone that aprons out

like a wave or a ski jump.
You who view us say

we look like a puzzle—
but we prefer to show

our own capacity to link.

George S. Chappell

This poetry collection is the author's first publication. George has been involved in writing for most of his adult life as an English teacher and a journalist. A recent recipient of a Master of Fine Arts from Goddard College in Plainfield, Vermont, he also has a Master of Arts in Folklore from the University of Pennsylvania and a BA in History from the University of Maine in Orono. A Quaker, he is a graduate of Moses Brown School, a Society of Friends school in Providence, R.I. He lives in Camden, Maine, where he participates in nearby poetry groups.

Notes

A FRESH FOOTPATH

10428257R00058

Made in the USA
Charleston, SC
03 December 2011